CHANGES

Written by **Marjorie N. Allen** and **Shelley Rotner**

Photographs by **Shelley Rotner**

Macmillan/McGraw-Hill School Publishing Company

New York   Chicago   Columbus

The photographs for this book were taken on 35mm Kodachrome film
and reproduced from color transparencies.

For information regarding permission, write to
Macmillan Publishing Company, 866 Third Avenue,
New York, NY 10022. Collier Macmillan Canada, Inc.,
1200 Eglinton Avenue East, Suite 200, Don Mills,
Ontario M3C 3N1.

This edition is reprinted by arrangement with
Macmillan Publishing Company, a division of Macmillan, Inc.

Macmillan/McGraw-Hill School Division
10 Union Square East, New York, New York 10003

Printed in the United States of America

ISBN 0-02-179069-8 / K. U.13

        4   5   6   7   8   9   BCM   99   98   97   96

All things go through changes

as they grow.

From fiddleheads to uncurled ferns,

scattered pinecones — forest tall;

flowers peek through one last snow

as winter's gray turns to green.

Milkweed clusters bloom in spring;

and feathered seeds in autumn
dance lightly in the wind.

Sun gives way to clouds,
clouds and wind to rain,

and winter's cold brings
ice and snow.

Seasons change—

leaves fall.

Spring blossoms yield summer fruit;

in autumn, corn grows high.

All things change,

then change again.

From fragile eggs

to birds

in flight,

from spotted fawn to great-horned buck,

and piglet small

to giant sow.

Horses, too — foal to mare.

All things

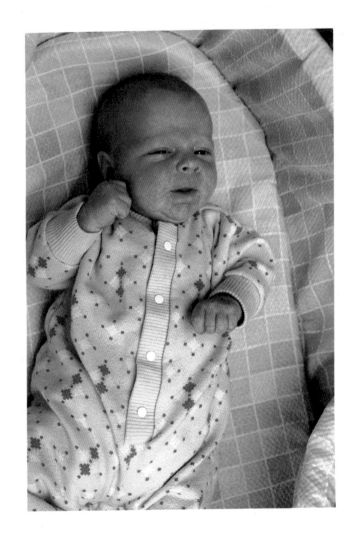

go through changes

as they grow.

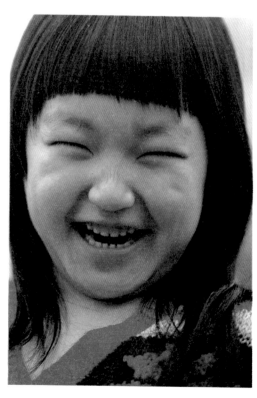